365 ways
to make the most of
your marriage

JULIET JANVRIN AND LUCY SELLECK

LION
Giftlines

To Bill   J.J.
To Stuart   L.S.

Text copyright © 2001 Juliet Janvrin and Lucy Selleck
Illustrations copyright © 2001 Stephanie Strickland
This edition copyright © 2001 Lion Publishing

The moral rights of the authors and illustrator
have been asserted

Published by
Lion Publishing plc
Sandy Lane West, Oxford, England
www.lion-publishing.co.uk
ISBN 0 7459 4720 4

First edition 2001
10 9 8 7 6 5 4 3 2 1 0

Acknowledgments

Page 3: quoted from The Alternative Service Book 1980,
copyright © The English Language Liturgical Consultation
(ELLC) and reproduced by permission of the publishers.

A catalogue record for this book is available
from the British Library

Typeset in 20/20 Kidprint
Printed and bound in Malta

To have and to hold
from this day forward;
for better, for worse,
for richer, for poorer,
in sickness and in health,
to love and to cherish,
till death us do part.

CHURCH MARRIAGE CEREMONY

Spring

👎 **1** 👍

Marriage, according to the law
of the country, is the union of one man
with one woman voluntarily entered into
for life to the exclusion of all others.

CIVIL MARRIAGE CEREMONY

👎 2 👍

The early days of marriage are full
of surprises – some nice, some nasty!

👎 3 👍

Planning a wedding is like rolling a
snowball down a hill: it gathers momentum.

👎 4 👍

The wedding day is important, but it is
nevertheless only one day in what you hope
will be a long and lasting relationship.

👎5👍

Spring is about new beginnings,
green shoots of hope for the future.
Your marriage has just begun.

👎6👍

Remember that you were married
in the sight of God. Let his gaze
rest on and bless your marriage.

👎 **7** 👍

Marriage is a lifelong commitment.
You stand before your nearest and
dearest and declare your long-term
intention to grow old beside another.

👎 **8** 👍

Masks don't work in marriage.
Be real, be vulnerable and without facade.

👎 **9** 👍

Marriage is like building a house.
Laying the foundations often means
digging tough ground.

👎 **10** 👍

Have independent friendships,
and share the interests and gains.

👎 **11** 👍

Don't always dump the dross of your day,
however broad the shoulders.

👎 **12** 👍

Realize that no one in this world
can fulfil all your needs and longings.

👎 **13** 👍

Contrary to popular belief,
love can mean having to say you're sorry!

👎 **14** 👍

Get home early from the office
and plan a treat together.

👎 15 👍
Keep your promises,
or don't make them.

👎 16 👍
Be a good timekeeper.
Don't keep each other waiting.

👎 17 👍
We all hold onto our secrets, but
within marriage they are best let go.

👎18👍
Notice how your partner looks,
and offer compliments.

👎19👍
Timing is of the essence
when saying something important.

👎20👍
Compromise may be necessary at Christmas.
All families celebrate differently.

👎 **21** 👍

Saying sorry means
doing something differently in future.

👎 **22** 👍

Share your dreams – and nightmares!

👎 **23** 👍

Leave the emotional baggage from
other relationships on the threshold
of your marriage.

👎24👍

Acknowledge when you are angry.
Don't smoulder or sulk.

👎25👍

Deal with little things that annoy you
before they become big things.

👎26👍

Share your insecurities,
and find security in one another.

👎 27 👍
Plan and budget together.
Money is both people's responsibility.

👎 28 👍
Intimacy only comes with trust.

👎 29 👍
Behaving like a child is
asking to be treated like one.

☞30☜
Adjusting to married life can
take time and involve a lot of tension!

☞31☜
Sometimes you must put aside some
of the customs, ways and thinking of
the family you were raised in if you
are to form a new one together.

👎**32**👍

Dirty socks are never appealing.
Don't leave yours lying around!

👎**33**👍

In a division of loyalties between your
parents and your marriage partner, it is
right to choose your partner. Your parents
are the past, your partner is the future.

👎**34**👍

Don't let the sun go down on your anger.

👎 35 👍
High expectations may be hard to meet.

👎 36 👍
We all choose to spend our money in different ways, and this can cause divisions.

👎 37 👍
Whether you like it or not,
you marry into someone else's family.

👎38👎

Marriage is popular *because* it combines the maximum of temptation with the maximum of opportunity.

GEORGE BERNARD SHAW

👎39👎

Listening is the other half of talking.

👎40👍
Cupboards don't tidy nor freezers
defrost without human intervention.
Whose will it be?

👎41👍
Remember that your sexual needs
and desires will not always match up.
Be generous to one another.

👎42👍
Respect your spouse's hopes and dreams.

👎 43 👍

Respect the in-laws, even when it seems difficult. They raised the person you have chosen to spend the rest of your life with.

👎 44 👍

A child binds you together in new responsibilities and a shared future purpose.

👎45👍
New babies can threaten
the exclusivity of marriage.

👎46👍
It is wonderful to have someone
who shares our consuming interest
in our children.

👎 47 👍

Don't assume that your spouse's
need for time on their own is a rejection.
Everyone needs space for themselves.

👎 48 👍

Remember that your marriage is
not your parents' marriage, and your
partner is not your mother or father.

👎 49 👍

Cuddling can *be* enough to feel close.

👎 50 👍
Toddlers can invade your intimacy,
and are jealous for the attention
you would like to give one another.

👎 51 👍
Find a babysitter you can trust,
and get out and give each other time.

👎52👍
You may come from very different
family backgrounds, even cultures.
Time and understanding are needed
to bring your diversities together.

👎53👍
Sharing the joy our children bring
is a great unifying force.

👎 54 👍

Remember that everyone needs the
boiled-egg-and-soldiers treatment
once in a while!

👎 55 👍

Take responsibility for your own feelings.
It is easy to blame your partner.

👎 56 👍

Exhaustion strains the relationship
of the new parents.

👎 57 👍

Computers are a great advantage of modern life, but they can also take over. Know when to switch off!

👎 58 👍

Make it a priority to protect your marriage. Have your own private space away from the rest of the world.

👎 59 👍

Young children can test a marriage
with their persistent physical demands.
You both need a rest sometimes.

👎 60 👍

It is unreasonable to expect your
partner to change if you are not
prepared to make changes yourself.

👎 61 👍
Seduction should not be lost
after the honeymoon.

👎 62 👍
Get in the habit early on of using 'I feel'
statements rather than 'You are' statements.

👎 63 👍
Winning arguments does not
always achieve a happy marriage.

👎 64 👍
Family and friends can be a great support,
but don't ask them to take sides.

👎 65 👍
Goodbyes and hellos are always important.
Seek out your partner with a loving word
when you leave or arrive.

👎 66 👍
A shared faith enriches and sustains marriage.

👍 **67** 👍

It is a haven of security to see your partner across a crowded room of unknown partygoers.

👍 **68** 👍

Irrational jealousy corrodes trust. You may need to deal with the insecurities of the past that cause the possessiveness of the present.

👆69👍

Share your aspirations early on in your marriage. You need to know them.

👆70👍

First babies call for a radical change in matrimonial routine.

👆71👍

Housework builds up like layers of dust. Don't leave it all to one person.

👎 72 👍

'Do it yourself' tasks done together
do not always enhance your relationship,
let alone your home.

👎 73 👍

Mobile phones are a great way to
communicate, but make sure it's your
partner you're speaking to!

☞ 74 ☜
An excessive interest in sport
and a happy marriage rarely mix.

☞ 75 ☜
Decide which one of you is going to
be book-keeper and support them in it.

☞ 76 ☜
A row can clear the air – or fill it
with things only meant at the moment,
but which are difficult to forget.

👎**77**👍

Tell your partner if a licked lip makes you loving but a stroked stomach makes you squirm!

👎**78**👍

Being married doesn't stop us being attracted to other people, but it should stop us doing anything about it.

👎 79 👍

Let the minor irritations of matrimonial life wash over you, or you will drown in a sea of annoyance.

👎 80 👍

Get to know each other's weaknesses and strengths with money, and discuss your hopes and fears.

👎 81 👍
A love note left on the pillow
touches the heart.

👎 82 👍
Living with someone else and their habits
is a matter of compromise.

👎 83 👍
A bullying spouse puts down their partner
in order to feel better about themselves.

👍84👎

Sometimes when you have come through a matrimonial bad patch, you can ask 'what was that all about?' That is why it is worth staying until you are out the other side.

👍85👎

A lot of friction within marriage is a repeat performance of our parents' relationships. Watch out for the reruns!

👎86👍

Pleasing our partner should be
more important than pleasing our parents.
We are now adults in an adult relationship.

👎87👍

When your partner is saying something,
listen. Don't just think of what you are
going to say next.

👎**88**👍

Enjoy having different opinions.
We can't and shouldn't always
feel the same way.

👎**89**👍

When love flies out of the window
for a while, keep the window open
and marriage can survive.

👎90👍

Discuss the right way to
squeeze the toothpaste before
seeing your solicitor!

👍91👎

For in what stupid age or nation
Was marriage ever out of fashion?

SAMUEL BUTLER

Summer

👎 92 👍

Summer is about long days of light and energy. Families grow fast. Sometimes the heat of the sun, life's cares, can threaten a marriage with weariness and burnout.

👍 93 👍
A quick hug is better than none.

👍 94 👍
Be brave enough to say what you want, although it may sometimes be hard.

👍 95 👍
It takes a little time to enjoy a holiday together. Give it just that.

👎 **96** 👍

Be a sun to your partner.
Light up their day with a loving gesture.

👎 **97** 👍

Constant complaining can become
extremely tiring in any relationship.

👎 **98** 👍

Forgiveness allows us to leave yesterday
behind so that we can enjoy today.

👎 **99** 👍

Christmas needs advance planning
together in order to be a true time
of celebration – for everyone!

👎 **100** 👍
Touching is the first step.

👎 **101** 👍
Don't assume what your spouse
is thinking. Check it out.

👎102👍
'For richer, for poorer' is a tough one
when it's usually the latter.

👎103👍
Teenagers test any marriage,
however strong.

👎104👍
Let roles and responsibilities be
shared and flexible. Life does not
always go according to plan.

☞105☜

You married for better, for worse.
If you always celebrate the first,
then the second can usually take
care of itself.

☞106☜

Don't deny that there's a problem
if you know there is.

👎107👍

Be careful with each other's feelings. We are all more fragile than we seem.

👎108👍

Be generous in your attention to your partner. Don't slot them into your life as an added extra.

👎109👍
Throwing things breaks more than plates.

👎110👍
Young people need the strength
of a united parental front.

👎111👍
If you have a past that is affecting
your marriage, then it is your responsibility
to deal with it, not your partner's. There
are people who can help.

👎 112 👍

Discuss and plan the family finances together. Two heads are better than one.

👎 113 👍

God is the third strand that plaits a marriage together to make a strong rope able to withstand life's tensions.

👎 114 👍
Hurts shared are more likely
to go away.

👎 115 👍
Don't assume there will be a
tomorrow in your marriage if you
take your spouse for granted today.

👎116👍
Adultery always begins with one small step,
one small incline along a rocky path.

👎117👍
Look after yourself.
Stress leaves little time for each other.

👎118👍
Spontaneous sex is wonderful,
but regular love-making sustains a marriage.

👎 119 👍
Beware of the friend who gives
unsolicited criticism about your partner.

👎 120 👍
Move on. Don't harbour grudges
and resentments.

👎 121 👍
Debt can overwhelm a marriage.
Try to avoid it.

👎 **122** 👍

A marriage is like a bank balance.
They both need regular investment.

👎 **123** 👍

Try to talk openly about a problem
without blaming the other person.

👎 **124** 👍

Busy careers and lifestyles can
be habit-forming. Break the habits
once in a while.

👎 **125** 👍

Rainy days happen in everyone's life.
Put something aside for them.

👎 **126** 👍

Car journeys are not the best time
to corner your partner!

👎127👍

Be careful. Over-controlling your partner
may lead to a break for freedom.

👎128👍

Any bereavement can rock a marriage,
and the death of a child can devastate it.
Seek help in your pain.

👎 129 👍

Moving house is stressful at the best of times. Try not to do it at the worst.

👎 130 👍

Planning holidays can often be more fun than going on them!

👎 131 👍

Facing concerns about children together is a great comfort.

👎 **132** 👍

Give your partner the choice of
doing a special activity they enjoy.

👎 **133** 👍

Where there is a joint will to save
a marriage, then there is a way.

👎 **134** 👍

Back up your partner when disciplining
children, even when you don't agree.
Tackle the issues later.

☞135☜
Addictive behaviour wrecks marriages and family life, but there is a cure and help for those who seek it.

☞136☜
Think about renewing your wedding vows every decade. God will bless that recommitment.

☞137☜
Change the venue. It's very refreshing.

👎138👍
Exercising together improves
body, mood and relationship.

👎139👍
Remember that a job is not
always for life, but your marriage is.

👎140👍
Parents who love each other provide
the best foundation for raising children.

👎 141 👍

Support and encourage your partner in their career. Let your confidence in them travel with them into the workplace.

👎 142 👍

Wealth is not important, but money worries are.

👎143👍

A spouse who is not contributing
properly to a marriage, whether
physically, emotionally or financially,
puts a strain on their partner.

👎144👍

If your marriage is in trouble,
seek help sooner rather than later.

👍145👎
Recognize emotional and physical
exhaustion in each other.

👍146👎
Infertility causes much pain and adjustment
to the expectations of a marriage that
yearned for children.

👍147👎
Rows can be like a runaway train.
Know where the brakes are, and use them!

☞ **148** 👍
We need to be looked after
when we are feeling unwell.

☞ **149** 👍
You may have to face the fact
that your marriage does not meet your
expectations. But were your expectations
reasonable in the first place?

👍 **150** 👎
Yes, a romantic dinner for two
does often end up with a passionate
night in *bed*!

👍 **151** 👎
Share the everyday happenings
with your partner every day.

👎 152 👍

The deceit of unfaithfulness is sometimes worse than the actions themselves.

👎 153 👍

Children don't have to hear your arguments to know that there is friction between you.

👎 **154** 👍

Remember that your marriage is a model for your children's future emotional relationships.

👎 **155** 👍

Teenagers remind you of your youth – and that neither of you are in it any longer!

👎156👍

Candles are cheap to come by,
and create a soft, romantic mood.

👎157👍

Accusations, anger and aggression
do not change people, but love and
understanding can.

👎158👍

Recognize that we all sometimes fail
to provide what the other person needs.

👎 **159** 👍

Build a portfolio of shared
memories to illuminate the
dark days of your marriage.

👎 **160** 👍

When other friends' marriages
fail, it makes our own marriage
vulnerable to attack.

🖓 1 6 1 👍

Holidays can *be* as stressful as the rest of life, if not planned properly.

🖓 1 6 2 👍

Listen and *be* attentive to your partner's concerns. Have you really heard what they said?

👎163👍

Showing you care can be as small as a favourite chocolate bar.

👎164👍

Wealth does not necessarily bring happiness to a marriage, but lack of it can bring unhappiness.

👎165👍

Tell each other if you don't understand – until you do!

👎166👍

Good friends enhance and strengthen your marriage. They do not seek to undermine it.

👎167👍

God is the cornerstone on which the house of marriage is built to withstand the storms of life.

👎168👍

Commit to saying at least one positive comment a day to your partner. We all need to hear good things about ourselves.

👎169👍

Trust can be quickly broken, but takes time to repair.

👎**170**👍

Shopping together only works
if you agree on what you like buying!

👎**171**👍

Create an oasis of matrimonial privacy
amongst the detritus of family life.

👎**172**👍

Getting on with each other's families
is a plus, but it is not always possible.

👎**173**👍
Adult behaviour inspires
an adult response.

👎**174**👍
It is easier to accept your
partner for who they are than
to try to change them.

👍 **175** 👍

Being kind to one another is
an act of will that becomes a habit.

👍 **176** 👍

A 'normal' sex life for you as a
couple is the one you have, as long
as you are both happy with it.

👎 177 👍
Home is not always the best
place to talk. Change the scenery.

👎 178 👍
Negative feelings can often
be overcome by choosing to
focus on the positive ones.

☞179☜
Sex can only improve if we tell
our partner what improves it for us.

☞180☜
God, the best maker of all marriages,
Combine your hearts in one.

WILLIAM SHAKESPEARE

Autumn

👎181👍

Autumn brings a slightly slower pace.
Children are growing up and leaving home.
This can be a new time of great colour
and intensity in a couple's life together.

👎182👍

Children leaving home closes a chapter
in your lives, but also opens new horizons.

👎183👍

The joys of marriage are the heaven on earth,
Life's paradise, great princess, the soul's quiet,
Sinews of concord, earthly immortality,
Eternity of pleasures, no restoratives
Like to a constant woman.

JOHN FORD

👎184👍

Marriage is ideally a meeting of
two minds, two bodies and two souls
in intimacy. Neglect any of these
areas and problems may ensue.

👎185👍

Have another honeymoon.
Go away for a night or two.

👎186👍
Old dreams may resurface or
new dreams emerge for both of you.
Be prepared to share them together.

👎187👍
Welcome different interests in
each other's lives, but not to the
detriment of your life together.

188

Looking at your marriage can be like looking at a painting. You need to stand back a little to get the whole view.

189

Buy a small present frequently, rather than a large one infrequently.

190

Change is like a torch that lightens the footpath to a different way.

👎191👍

The empty nest syndrome can
be balanced by plans to welcome
freedom from parental responsibility.

👎192👍

Put yourself in your husband or
wife's shoes. They do not always
feel as comfortable as your own.

👎193👍
Patience with one another when
you both want to be heard is difficult,
but there is time enough.

👎194👍
Needing some time alone is understandable.
Always wanting time alone is not.

👎195👍
Talking helps. Encourage one another.

👎196👍
Travel to destinations
you always wanted to go to.

👎197👍
Talk to each other on equal terms,
not as parent to child.

👎198👍
Share your sadness.
Your partner needs to know.

☞199☜
A wedding photograph sits on
the dressing table – a snapshot of
a promise. Commit to keeping it.

☞200☜
Light some candles,
and have a scented bath together.

201

Cook a favourite meal together,
and take time to enjoy it.

202

Keep your bedtime for calm
discussion. Don't turn it into
a place of acrimony.

203

Remember the pastimes you
both enjoyed, and revisit them.

204

Don't always be right. You're not, you know!

205

Admitting to one another that you are
wrong is hard, but comes with practice.

206
Soft words turn away angry feelings.
Hard words escalate conflict.

207
Don't swallow accumulated hurts.
They can grow into a well of rage.

208
Cuddles carry us through life's colder days.

👎 **209** 👍
Ask for help.
Don't carry the burden alone.

👎 **210** 👍
An enduring sexual relationship is built
on communication, acceptance, warmth
and friendship.

👎 **211** 👍
Adultery is usually a symptom
and not the cause of marriage malaise.

👎 **2 1 2** 👍
Emotional turmoil can *be* shared,
however much of a muddle it all seems!

👎 **2 1 3** 👍
Plan in a 'talk' time to spend together
each week. Prioritize it as the most important
non-negotiable appointment that you have.

👎 **2 1 4** 👍
Plan to revisit favourite courting places.

👎215👍
Not enough outside company
can *stultify* a marriage.

👎216👍
Sometimes we need to nurture
our partner like a good parent.

👎217👍
Like anything precious, marriage
should last a lifetime. Look after it!

👎218👍
Giving your partner a good lecture
does not make them a good student.

👎219👍
Don't leave skeletons locked in
the cupboard. Otherwise, when you
open it they will haunt you both.

👎220👍
Buy a treat for the partner
who is caring for a sick relative.

221

Unexpected events may force you
to reassess your life together.

222

Having separate friends and
interests is important, but should not
replace your friendship together.

👎 **223** 👍

Give some thought to unrealized
dreams. Some may be shared.
Some can be realized individually.

👎 **224** 👍

Children prefer to leave happy,
independent parents with a life
of their own. Have you got one?

👎 225 👍
Love comes in waves through marriage.
Like surfing, you sometimes have to wait
on a calm sea.

👎 226 👍
Tuning into each other's needs can
be difficult if the transmission is faulty.

👎 227 👍
Explore new ways of getting closer physically.
Have you let things drift in recent years?

☞228👍
New roles demand new ground rules.

☞229👎
Fear of confrontation can stop us sorting out difficult issues in our marriage, but lack of confrontation can lead to matrimonial breakdown.

👎 **230** 👍

Discuss change,
and what it means to each of you.

👎 **231** 👍

Romantic love is not enough.
Marriage is built on action
as well as emotion.

👎232👍
Swap those household tasks you have
always done. Give each other a break.

👎233👍
A critical spirit can create
a stranglehold on a marriage.

👎234👍
Sharing a good giggle is a great medicine.

👎 235 👍
Forgive and forget past wrongs –
again and again and again!

👎 236 👍
Contempt is a canker that opens
the door to matrimonial destruction.

👎 237 👍
Remember that it needs two
to engage in a dialogue.

👎238👍
Small, tender gestures touch us.

👎239👍
Listen to your partner with your
eyes as well as your ears. Eyes
are the doors to the heart.

👎240👍
Growth together only comes
if you both embrace it.

👎**2 4 1**👍

It is often hard to articulate changes in ourselves to our partners when we have not yet made sense of them.

👎**2 4 2**👍

No one else can make us happy. We can choose to seek our own happiness at whatever age and stage of life.

👎 **243** 👍
A close physical relationship
isn't just for the under-forties!
This is a time for renewal.

👎 **244** 👍
Affairs have a message to give
to a marriage, not necessarily that
it is over, but that all is not well
and that change is necessary.

👎245👍
Hobbies are a great way of relaxing,
but avoid them taking over your life
and marriage.

👎246👍
Interrupting means that your partner
cannot finish what they need to say.

👎247👍
If you have something important to say,
it is often how you say it, not what you say.

👎248👍
Look to each other to support,
not to blame.

👎249👍
Keeping sad feelings in
can create barriers between you.

👎250👍
Going out for a meal is
an opportunity to talk, not an
opportunity to sit in silence.

👎 2 5 1 👍
Take regular breaks,
even if they are short ones.

👎 2 5 2 👍
Promotion probably means longer hours.
Review household chores.

👎 2 5 3 👍
Surprise your partner with
something unexpected. Predictability
can lead to boredom.

👎**254**👍

A midlife crisis is a time of turbulence. Be tolerant of your partner if they seem to be in one!

👎**255**👍

Be flexible in your outlook during this new phase.

👎**256**👍

Exchange ideas for change you would like. Be prepared to accept each other's.

👎257👍
Tell each other if you don't understand.
Explain until the matter is clear to you both.

👎258👍
Pride in our grown children is
the enjoyment of a shared endeavour.

👎259👍
Love, acceptance and tolerance
are keynotes of the matrimonial tune.

👆260👇
Marriage is about a partnership,
and not a boardroom battle.

👆261👇
A long-lasting marriage is like being
wrapped in a security blanket. Hold it close.

👆262👇
Gossip after an evening out is one of the
pleasures of a married couple returning home.

👎263👍
Plant a plant that flowers at the same time as your wedding anniversary.

👎264👍
Pick up the phone and check out your partner's day. A loving voice is often a welcome respite.

👎265👍
Individual restlessness indicates that you need to make your marriage move on.

👎 266 👍

Remember your promise to
'cherish' your partner. Wrap them
in your warmth and affection.

👎 267 👍

Christmas can put an increasing strain
on a couple's marriage. Change the routine
and celebrate it differently this year.

👎**268**👍

A good relationship is about dependence in all its most positive sense. Lean on one another from time to time.

👎**269**👍

Ill-health and stress dampen the libido. You or your partner may have to wait patiently for restoration.

👎270👍

Don't soul-search and come to life-changing conclusions without mentioning the investigation to your partner!

👎271👍

A refining process can take place through the furnace of a good marriage that gradually eliminates the dross.

👎 **272** 👍

Help your partner look after their health.
You have an investment in their well-being.

👎 **273** 👍

The men that women marry
And why they marry them will always be
A marvel and mystery to the world.

HENRY WADSWORTH LONGFELLOW

Winter

👎**274**👍

Winter is about drawing the curtains
and staying warm inside. Your years
of commitment to one another are like
a well-made fire that glows against
the chill of old age.

👎 **275** 👍

Sitting in your favourite armchair every night is cosy, but share the sofa instead.

👎 **276** 👍

All love at first, like generous wine,
Ferments and frets until 'tis fine;
But when 'tis settled on the lee,
And from th' impurer matter free,
Becomes the richer still the older,
And proves the pleasanter the colder.

SAMUEL BUTLER

👎277👍

Bodies change, wrinkle and wither, but the beloved's eyes remain constant — a window to the person you fell in love with long ago.

👎278👍

Keep alive memories of courtship in special places, songs and letters.

👎279👍

We find growing old hard sometimes. Be sensitive to the changes in each other.

👎280👍

Don't allow hours of differences
to drift into days, months and years.
Address them – life is short!

👎281👍

New paths make way for new directions.
Try taking them together.

👎282👍

'In sickness and in health' – the former often
becomes a painful reality in our winter years.

👎283👍

Grandchildren recapture the spring
days of our children's youth – days
that we can remember together.

👎284👍

Aches and pains become an interesting topic
of conversation to the more mature couple!

👎285👍

A present without a reason
is a good reason to give one.

👎**286**👍

As it matures, companionship becomes one of the most important and valued components of married life.

👉**287**👍

When our partner is in pain, we feel helpless.

👉**288**👍

We all suffer from periods of emotional vulnerability, and need extra sensitivity and care.

☜289☞
Marriage is like a lifelong investment.
Dividends grow and mature, and are
paid out in the later years.

☜290☞
A mature and loving marriage is like
the sweetness of a much loved melody.

☜291☞
A mature but embittered marriage is
a twisted cacophony of sound.

☞**292**👍

Gardening together opens up the doors of your marriage. Plan who does different tasks, so that you don't tread on each other's welly boots!

☞**293**👍

Change is difficult, but it can also be the road to pastures new.

☞**294**👍

Remember the words 'I love you.'

👎 **295** 👍

Tolerance of each other's faults results
in a gentle and heartwarming acceptance
that allows give-and-take.

👎 **296** 👍

Tell your husband and wife how much
they have meant to you, before it is too late.

👎 **297** 👍

Sharing grandchildren is one of the
great blessings of a long-lived marriage.

👎298👍
Nursing a failing partner is very hard.

👎299👍
The more you have had to work at a marriage, the more you can appreciate its long-term endurance.

👎300👍
Reassure yourself, in times of doubt, when your partner is gravely ill, that you can only do your best.

👎301👍

The ageing body causes insecurity. We all need reassurance to deal with a changing shape and a skin that seems too big!

👎302👍

Retirement brings with it mixed blessings. Count those blessings, but be flexible with the changes.

👎303👍

Just holding hands creates warmth.

👍304👎

Wisdom in later life is a very useful resource. Tap into it in your marriage.

👎305👍

They say old habits never die, but some need to do just that. Breaking the habits of a lifetime allows new ideas to develop.

👍306👍

We never stop learning new things about our partner.

☞307☜
A cup of tea together is
a comfort at any time of day.

☞308☜
Part of the art of negotiation is
the willingness to compromise.

☞309☜
Remember that the carer as well
as the patient needs attention when
one of you is sick.

👎310👍

Interest and involvement in the younger
generation keep us in the flow of life.

👎311👍

A glass of wine, a takeaway and an
old film you saw together in the cinema
long ago equals happy relaxation.

👎312👍

Old friends buoy up old marriages
like a welcome float.

👎313👍
Hearing the same stories retold gets easier as you become more forgetful yourself!

👎314👍
We may need to be the eyes or ears of our partner in old age.

👎315👍
Marriages and people change over the years together. What you did understand about each other, you may not now.

👎316👍
Look back in the photograph album at happy days. It can be lovely to reminisce.

👎317👍
The time and experience you have together in your later years give you the tools for when things get tough.

👎318👍
Give your partner something that represents the best in your marriage.

☞319☜
Silence is golden.
Enjoy the peace and quiet between you.

☞320☜
Going to bed at different times
can become a lifelong habit. Break it
once in a while and have a cuddle.

☞321☜
Routine is a good anchor, but can become
monotonous. Change it and enjoy the fresh air.

👎322👍
Stay in bed together one day, open a box of your favourite chocolates and relax. You're allowed to be indulgent in your old age!

👎323👍
The marriages of our children are full of their own emotions. Stay clear of interfering and trying to resolve things for them.

👎324👍
Age and time need not destroy love.

👎**325**👍

A walk together can be
a wonderful shared pleasure.

👎**326**👍

Having and holding are the
alpha and omega of marriage.

👎**327**👍

As the years go by, it is easy
to lose sight of the first time
you set eyes upon each other.

👎**328**👍

The changes of old age may
change the balance of your marriage.

👎**329**👍

Have a laugh together. Humour
is the bedrock of a long marriage.

👎**330**👍

Celebrate your wedding anniversary.
Your marriage is an achievement!

👎331👍
Creating change in your relationship
can add new depth and colour.

👎332👍
Just hearing your partner's problems
is helpful. There is not always a solution.

👎333👍
A person who is grieving needs to
talk it through. Give your partner time.

👎334👍
Words written in a love letter resonate down the years in a way that spoken words cannot.

👎335👍
When we are older, we are often too proud to seek help. It is then that we need to be sure that we have nothing further to learn.

👎336👍
Put things to look forward to in your diary, and anticipate them together.

👎337👍
None of us wants to be patronized by our nearest and dearest, even if we have been together for half a lifetime!

👎338👍
It is peculiar how the irritating traits of yesteryear can become endearingly familiar after long years of acquaintance.

👎339👍
Inside a frailer body is the same lover.

☞**340**☝

Your grandchildren and great-grandchildren are a reminder of how your marriage will continue to be a part of future generations.

☞**341**☝

The difficulties of old age can be irritating to a partner who is not suffering from that particular one!

☞**342**☝

When old friends die, it is a bitter blow.

👎**343**👍

Having arms wrapped round you
is often more important than sex.

👎**344**👍

Discuss what dying means to you,
and help your partner to prepare.

👎**345**👍

A good marriage is like a harbour that
you have returned to again and again
after a life of journeys on the open sea.

👎**346**👍
If our partner loses their mind, it is
as if they have left us to go to another
land. The pain can be immense.

👎**347**👍
Music has many moods. So does love-making.

👎**348**👍
Find out what turns your partner on –
and turn it on. Sometimes what we enjoy
changes as we get older!

👎349👍
Switch the TV off
and put your favourite old music on.

👎350👍
Good sex is not the prerogative of the young,
although they would like us to think so!

👎351👍
Marriage is not like an automatic car.
You have to change gear to get somewhere,
even in the later years.

👎**352**👍

It is a great relaxation to be with
a person who has seen you grow and
mature throughout a lifetime – and
loved you through it!

👎**353**👍

The last and one of the most loving things
you may be able to do for your husband
or wife is to sit and hold their hand.

👎354👍

In a happy marriage it is the
wife who provides the climate,
the husband the landscape.

GERALD BRENAN

👎355👍

It is good to see other couples,
old friends, who have endured
as we have.

👎356👍

Redecorate your bedroom to be
as you have always wanted it. Make
it a special haven for you both.

👎357👍

A lifelong partner is like a watchmaker
who knows just how the cogwheels turn
within your head.

👎358👍

Count your blessings together.

👎**359**👍

Fear of loss can colour the late
days of marriage. Enjoy and savour
your time together.

👎**360**👍

Each day, reflect on a happy day
that you remember from the past.

👎**361**👍

The devotion of one for another is grace
from God combined with human endeavour.

362

A long marriage is a blessing,
not just to those who have lived it,
but to their children and their
children's children.

363

When all else fades away, a long
marriage is a testimony of the
endurance of loving human relationship
that reflects the eternity of the soul.

☞364☜

While there is life and energy,
be as energetic as you both can be.

☞365☜

To every marriage there are seasons –
spring, summer, autumn and winter. To each
and every season life will bring its own joy,
happiness, sadness and difficulties. If a
husband and wife face these united, with
faces turned towards one another, then
God will surely bless their embrace.